In Loving Memory Of

_____

Date

_____

Gone But Not Forgotten

Gone But Not Forgotten

Guests

Name

Email and number

Address

Favourite Memory

Name

Email and number

Adress

Favourite Memory

Name

Email and number

Adress

Favourite Memory

Guests

Name

Email and number

Address

Favourite Memory

Name

Email and number

Adress

Favourite Memory

Name

Email and number

Adress

Favourite Memory

Guests

Name
_____

Email and number
_____

Address
_____

Favourite Memory
_____

_____

_____

Name
_____

Email and number
_____

Adress
_____

Favourite Memory
_____

_____

_____

Name
_____

Email and number
_____

Adress
_____

Favourite Memory
_____

_____

_____

Guests

Name _____

Email and number _____

Address _____
_____

Favourite Memory _____
_____
_____
_____

Name _____

Email and number _____

Adress _____
_____

Favourite Memory _____
_____
_____
_____

Name _____

Email and number _____

Adress _____
_____

Favourite Memory _____
_____
_____
_____

Guests

Name

Email and number

Address

Favourite Memory

Name

Email and number

Adress

Favourite Memory

Name

Email and number

Adress

Favourite Memory

Guests

Name
_____

Email and number
_____

Address
_____

_____

Name
_____

Email and number
_____

Adress
_____

_____

Name
_____

Email and number
_____

Adress
_____

_____

Favourite Memory
_____

_____

_____

_____

Favourite Memory
_____

_____

_____

_____

Favourite Memory
_____

_____

_____

Guests

Name _____

Email and number _____

Address _____

Favourite Memory _____
_____
_____

Name _____

Email and number _____

Adress _____

Favourite Memory _____
_____
_____

Name _____

Email and number _____

Adress _____

Favourite Memory _____
_____
_____

Guests

Name
_____

Email and number
_____

Address
_____
_____

Name
_____

Email and number
_____

Adress
_____
_____

Name
_____

Email and number
_____

Adress
_____
_____

Favourite Memory
_____
_____
_____
_____

Favourite Memory
_____
_____
_____
_____

Favourite Memory
_____
_____
_____
_____

Guests

Name

Favourite Memory

Email and number

Address

Name

Favourite Memory

Email and number

Adress

Name

Favourite Memory

Email and number

Adress

Guests

Name

Email and number

Address

Name

Email and number

Adress

Name

Email and number

Adress

Favourite Memory

Favourite Memory

Favourite Memory

Guests

Name _____

Email and number _____

Address _____

Favourite Memory _____
_____
_____
_____

Name _____

Email and number _____

Adress _____

Favourite Memory _____
_____
_____
_____

Name _____

Email and number _____

Adress _____

Favourite Memory _____
_____
_____
_____

Guests

Name

Email and number

Address

Favourite Memory

Name

Email and number

Adress

Favourite Memory

Name

Email and number

Adress

Favourite Memory

Guests

Name

Email and number

Address

Favourite Memory

Name

Email and number

Adress

Favourite Memory

Name

Email and number

Adress

Favourite Memory

Guests

Name
_____

Email and number
_____

Address
_____
_____

Name
_____

Email and number
_____

Adress
_____
_____

Name
_____

Email and number
_____

Adress
_____
_____

Favourite Memory
_____
_____
_____
_____

Favourite Memory
_____
_____
_____
_____

Favourite Memory
_____
_____
_____
_____

Guests

Name _____

Email and number _____

Address _____

_____

Name _____

Email and number _____

Adress _____

_____

Name _____

Email and number _____

Adress _____

_____

Favourite Memory _____

_____

_____

_____

Favourite Memory _____

_____

_____

_____

Favourite Memory _____

_____

_____

Guests

Name _____

Email and number _____

Address _____
_____

Name _____

Email and number _____

Adress _____
_____

Name _____

Email and number _____

Adress _____
_____

Favourite Memory _____
_____
_____
_____

Favourite Memory _____
_____
_____
_____

Favourite Memory _____
_____
_____

Guests

Name
_____

Email and number
_____

Address
_____
_____

Name
_____

Email and number
_____

Adress
_____
_____

Name
_____

Email and number
_____

Adress
_____

Favourite Memory
_____
_____
_____

Favourite Memory
_____
_____
_____

Favourite Memory
_____
_____

Guests

Name

Email and number

Address

Name

Email and number

Adress

Name

Email and number

Adress

Favourite Memory

Favourite Memory

Favourite Memory

Guests

Name

Favourite Memory

Email and number

Address

Name

Favourite Memory

Email and number

Adress

Name

Favourite Memory

Email and number

Adress

Guests

Name
_____

Email and number
_____

Address
_____

_____

Name
_____

Email and number
_____

Adress
_____

_____

Name
_____

Email and number
_____

Adress
_____

_____

Favourite Memory
_____

_____

_____

Favourite Memory
_____

_____

_____

Favourite Memory
_____

_____

_____

Guests

Name

Email and number

Address

Name

Email and number

Adress

Name

Email and number

Adress

Favourite Memory

Favourite Memory

Favourite Memory

Guests

Name
_____

Email and number
_____

Address
_____

_____

Name
_____

Email and number
_____

Adress
_____

_____

Name
_____

Email and number
_____

Adress
_____

_____

Favourite Memory
_____

_____

_____

_____

Favourite Memory
_____

_____

_____

_____

Favourite Memory
_____

_____

_____

_____

Guests

Name
_____

Email and number
_____

Address
_____

Favourite Memory
_____

_____

_____

Name
_____

Email and number
_____

Adress
_____

Favourite Memory
_____

_____

_____

Name
_____

Email and number
_____

Adress
_____

Favourite Memory
_____

_____

_____

Guests

Name

Favourite Memory

Email and number

Address

Name

Favourite Memory

Email and number

Adress

Name

Favourite Memory

Email and number

Adress

Guests

Name

Email and number

Address

Name

Email and number

Adress

Name

Email and number

Adress

Favourite Memory

Favourite Memory

Favourite Memory

Guests

Name

Email and number

Address

Name

Email and number

Adress

Name

Email and number

Adress

Favourite Memory

Favourite Memory

Favourite Memory

Guests

Name

Email and number

Address

Favourite Memory

Name

Email and number

Adress

Favourite Memory

Name

Email and number

Adress

Favourite Memory

Guests

Name

Email and number

Address

Name

Email and number

Adress

Name

Email and number

Adress

Favourite Memory

Favourite Memory

Favourite Memory

Guests

Name

Email and number

Address

Favourite Memory

Name

Email and number

Adress

Favourite Memory

Name

Email and number

Adress

Favourite Memory

Guests

Name
_____

Email and number
_____

Address
_____
_____

Favourite Memory
_____
_____
_____
_____

Name
_____

Email and number
_____

Adress
_____
_____

Favourite Memory
_____
_____
_____
_____

Name
_____

Email and number
_____

Adress
_____
_____

Favourite Memory
_____
_____
_____
_____

Guests

Name

Email and number

Address

Name

Email and number

Adress

Name

Email and number

Adress

Favourite Memory

Favourite Memory

Favourite Memory

Guests

Name

Email and number

Address

Favourite Memory

Name

Email and number

Adress

Favourite Memory

Name

Email and number

Adress

Favourite Memory

Guests

Name

Favourite Memory

Email and number

Address

Name

Favourite Memory

Email and number

Adress

Name

Favourite Memory

Email and number

Adress

Guests

Name
_____

Email and number
_____

Address
_____

_____

Name
_____

Email and number
_____

Adress
_____

_____

Name
_____

Email and number
_____

Adress
_____

_____

Favourite Memory
_____

_____

_____

_____

Favourite Memory
_____

_____

_____

_____

Favourite Memory
_____

_____

_____

Guests

Name

Favourite Memory

Email and number

Address

Name

Favourite Memory

Email and number

Adress

Name

Favourite Memory

Email and number

Adress

Guests

Name _____

Email and number _____

Address _____

_____

Name _____

Email and number _____

Adress _____

_____

Name _____

Email and number _____

Adress _____

_____

Favourite Memory _____

_____

_____

_____

Favourite Memory _____

_____

_____

_____

Favourite Memory _____

_____

_____

_____

Guests

Name

Favourite Memory

Email and number

Address

Name

Favourite Memory

Email and number

Adress

Name

Favourite Memory

Email and number

Adress

Guests

Name
_____

Email and number
_____

Address
_____

_____

Name
_____

Email and number
_____

Adress
_____

_____

Name
_____

Email and number
_____

Adress
_____

_____

Favourite Memory
_____

_____

_____

_____

Favourite Memory
_____

_____

_____

_____

Favourite Memory
_____

_____

_____

_____

Guests

Name
_____

Email and number
_____

Address
_____

_____

Favourite Memory
_____

_____

_____

_____

Name
_____

Email and number
_____

Adress
_____

_____

Favourite Memory
_____

_____

_____

_____

Name
_____

Email and number
_____

Adress
_____

_____

Favourite Memory
_____

_____

_____

_____

Guests

Name _____

Email and number _____

Address _____

_____

Favourite Memory _____

_____

_____

_____

Name _____

Email and number _____

Adress _____

_____

Favourite Memory _____

_____

_____

_____

Name _____

Email and number _____

Adress _____

_____

Favourite Memory _____

_____

_____

_____

Guests

Name

Email and number

Address

Favourite Memory

Name

Email and number

Adress

Favourite Memory

Name

Email and number

Adress

Favourite Memory

Guests

Name

Email and number

Address

Name

Email and number

Adress

Name

Email and number

Adress

Favourite Memory

Favourite Memory

Favourite Memory

Guests

Name
_____

Email and number
_____

Address
_____

Favourite Memory
_____
_____
_____

Name
_____

Email and number
_____

Adress
_____

Favourite Memory
_____
_____
_____

Name
_____

Email and number
_____

Adress
_____

Favourite Memory
_____
_____
_____

Guests

Name _____

Email and number _____

Address _____

_____

Name _____

Email and number _____

Adress _____

_____

Name _____

Email and number _____

Adress _____

_____

Favourite Memory _____

_____

_____

_____

Favourite Memory _____

_____

_____

_____

Favourite Memory _____

_____

_____

Guests

Name

Email and number

Address

Favourite Memory

Name

Email and number

Adress

Favourite Memory

Name

Email and number

Adress

Favourite Memory

Guests

Name

Email and number

Address

Favourite Memory

Name

Email and number

Adress

Favourite Memory

Name

Email and number

Adress

Favourite Memory

Guests

Name

Email and number

Address

Favourite Memory

Name

Email and number

Adress

Favourite Memory

Name

Email and number

Adress

Favourite Memory

Guests

Name

Email and number

Address

Favourite Memory

Name

Email and number

Adress

Favourite Memory

Name

Email and number

Adress

Favourite Memory

Guests

Name _____

Email and number _____

Address _____

Favourite Memory _____
_____
_____
_____

Name _____

Email and number _____

Adress _____

Favourite Memory _____
_____
_____
_____

Name _____

Email and number _____

Adress _____

Favourite Memory _____
_____
_____

Guests

Name

Email and number

Address

Name

Email and number

Adress

Name

Email and number

Adress

Favourite Memory

Favourite Memory

Favourite Memory

Guests

Name _____

Email and number _____

Address _____

Name _____

Email and number _____

Adress _____

Name _____

Email and number _____

Adress _____

Favourite Memory _____

_____

_____

Favourite Memory _____

_____

_____

Favourite Memory _____

_____

_____

Guests

Name

Favourite Memory

Email and number

Address

Name

Favourite Memory

Email and number

Adress

Name

Favourite Memory

Email and number

Adress

Guests

Name
_____

Email and number
_____

Address
_____

Favourite Memory
_____

_____

_____

Name
_____

Email and number
_____

Adress
_____

Favourite Memory
_____

_____

_____

Name
_____

Email and number
_____

Adress
_____

Favourite Memory
_____

_____

_____

Guests

Name
_____

Email and number
_____

Address
_____
_____

Name
_____

Email and number
_____

Adress
_____
_____

Name
_____

Email and number
_____

Adress
_____
_____

Favourite Memory
_____
_____
_____
_____

Favourite Memory
_____
_____
_____
_____

Favourite Memory
_____
_____
_____

Guests

Name

Email and number

Address

Favourite Memory

Name

Email and number

Adress

Favourite Memory

Name

Email and number

Adress

Favourite Memory

Guests

Name

Email and number

Address

Favourite Memory

Name

Email and number

Adress

Favourite Memory

Name

Email and number

Adress

Favourite Memory

Guests

Name

Email and number

Address

Favourite Memory

Name

Email and number

Adress

Favourite Memory

Name

Email and number

Adress

Favourite Memory

Guests

Name

Email and number

Address

Name

Email and number

Adress

Name

Email and number

Adress

Favourite Memory

Favourite Memory

Favourite Memory

Guests

Name
_____

Email and number
_____

Address
_____

Favourite Memory
_____
_____
_____
_____

Name
_____

Email and number
_____

Adress
_____

Favourite Memory
_____
_____
_____
_____

Name
_____

Email and number
_____

Adress
_____

Favourite Memory
_____
_____
_____
_____

Guests

Name

Email and number

Address

Favourite Memory

Name

Email and number

Adress

Favourite Memory

Name

Email and number

Adress

Favourite Memory

Guests

Name

Email and number

Address

Favourite Memory

Name

Email and number

Adress

Favourite Memory

Name

Email and number

Adress

Favourite Memory

Guests

Name

Email and number

Address

Favourite Memory

Name

Email and number

Adress

Favourite Memory

Name

Email and number

Adress

Favourite Memory

Guests

Name

Favourite Memory

Email and number

Address

Name

Favourite Memory

Email and number

Adress

Name

Favourite Memory

Email and number

Adress

Guests

Name
_____

Email and number
_____

Address
_____

_____

Favourite Memory
_____

_____

_____

_____

Name
_____

Email and number
_____

Adress
_____

_____

Favourite Memory
_____

_____

_____

_____

Name
_____

Email and number
_____

Adress
_____

_____

Favourite Memory
_____

_____

_____

_____

Guests

Name

Email and number

Address

Favourite Memory

Name

Email and number

Adress

Favourite Memory

Name

Email and number

Adress

Favourite Memory

Guests

Name
_____

Email and number
_____

Address
_____

_____

Name
_____

Email and number
_____

Adress
_____

_____

Name
_____

Email and number
_____

Adress
_____

_____

Favourite Memory
_____

_____

_____

_____

Favourite Memory
_____

_____

_____

_____

Favourite Memory
_____

_____

_____

Guests

Name _____

Email and number _____

Address _____
_____

Favourite Memory _____
_____
_____
_____

Name _____

Email and number _____

Adress _____
_____

Favourite Memory _____
_____
_____

Name _____

Email and number _____

Adress _____
_____

Favourite Memory _____
_____
_____

Guests

Name

Email and number

Address

Favourite Memory

Name

Email and number

Adress

Favourite Memory

Name

Email and number

Adress

Favourite Memory

Guests

Name   Favourite Memory
_____   _____
Email and number
_____   _____
Address
_____   _____
_____   _____

Name   Favourite Memory
_____   _____
Email and number
_____   _____
Adress
_____   _____
_____   _____

Name   Favourite Memory
_____   _____
Email and number
_____   _____
Adress
_____   _____
_____   _____

Guests

Name

Email and number

Address

Name

Email and number

Adress

Name

Email and number

Adress

Favourite Memory

Favourite Memory

Favourite Memory

Guests

Name

Email and number

Address

Favourite Memory

Name

Email and number

Adress

Favourite Memory

Name

Email and number

Adress

Favourite Memory

Guests

Name

Email and number

Address

Name

Email and number

Adress

Name

Email and number

Adress

Favourite Memory

Favourite Memory

Favourite Memory

Guests

Name

Email and number

Address

Favourite Memory

Name

Email and number

Adress

Favourite Memory

Name

Email and number

Adress

Favourite Memory

Guests

Name
_____

Email and number
_____

Address
_____
_____

Name
_____

Email and number
_____

Adress
_____
_____

Name
_____

Email and number
_____

Adress
_____
_____

Favourite Memory
_____
_____
_____
_____

Favourite Memory
_____
_____
_____
_____

Favourite Memory
_____
_____
_____

Guests

Name

Email and number

Address

Favourite Memory

Name

Email and number

Adress

Favourite Memory

Name

Email and number

Adress

Favourite Memory

Guests

Name	Favourite Memory
Email and number	
Address	

Name	Favourite Memory
Email and number	
Adress	

Name	Favourite Memory
Email and number	
Adress	

Guests

Name

Email and number

Address

Favourite Memory

Name

Email and number

Adress

Favourite Memory

Name

Email and number

Adress

Favourite Memory

Guests

Name
_____

Email and number
_____

Address
_____
_____

Name
_____

Email and number
_____

Adress
_____
_____

Name
_____

Email and number
_____

Adress
_____
_____

Favourite Memory
_____
_____
_____

Favourite Memory
_____
_____
_____

Favourite Memory
_____
_____
_____

Guests

Name

Email and number

Address

Favourite Memory

Name

Email and number

Adress

Favourite Memory

Name

Email and number

Adress

Favourite Memory

Guests

Name

Email and number

Address

Name

Email and number

Adress

Name

Email and number

Adress

Favourite Memory

Favourite Memory

Favourite Memory

Guests

Name

Favourite Memory

Email and number

Address

Name

Favourite Memory

Email and number

Adress

Name

Favourite Memory

Email and number

Adress

Guests

Name

Email and number

Address

Name

Email and number

Adress

Name

Email and number

Adress

Favourite Memory

Favourite Memory

Favourite Memory

Guests

Name

Email and number

Address

Favourite Memory

Name

Email and number

Adress

Favourite Memory

Name

Email and number

Adress

Favourite Memory

Guests

Name

Email and number

Address

Name

Email and number

Adress

Name

Email and number

Adress

Favourite Memory

Favourite Memory

Favourite Memory

Guests

Name _____

Email and number _____

Address _____

_____

Name _____

Email and number _____

Adress _____

_____

Name _____

Email and number _____

Adress _____

Favourite Memory _____

_____

_____

Favourite Memory _____

_____

_____

Favourite Memory _____

_____

Guests

Name

Email and number

Address

Favourite Memory

Name

Email and number

Adress

Favourite Memory

Name

Email and number

Adress

Favourite Memory

Guests

Name
_____

Email and number
_____

Address
_____

Favourite Memory
_____
_____
_____
_____

Name
_____

Email and number
_____

Adress
_____

Favourite Memory
_____
_____
_____
_____

Name
_____

Email and number
_____

Adress
_____

Favourite Memory
_____
_____
_____

Guests

Name _____

Email and number _____

Address _____

_____

Favourite Memory _____

_____

_____

_____

Name _____

Email and number _____

Adress _____

_____

Favourite Memory _____

_____

_____

_____

Name _____

Email and number _____

Adress _____

_____

Favourite Memory _____

_____

_____

Guests

Name

Email and number

Address

Favourite Memory

Name

Email and number

Adress

Favourite Memory

Name

Email and number

Adress

Favourite Memory

Guests

Name
_____

Email and number
_____

Address
_____

_____

Name
_____

Email and number
_____

Adress
_____

_____

Name
_____

Email and number
_____

Adress
_____

_____

Favourite Memory
_____

_____

_____

_____

Favourite Memory
_____

_____

_____

_____

Favourite Memory
_____

_____

_____

_____

Guests

Name

Email and number

Address

Name

Email and number

Adress

Name

Email and number

Adress

Favourite Memory

Favourite Memory

Favourite Memory

Guests

Name

Email and number

Address

Favourite Memory

Name

Email and number

Adress

Favourite Memory

Name

Email and number

Adress

Favourite Memory

Guests

Name

Email and number

Address

Favourite Memory

Name

Email and number

Adress

Favourite Memory

Name

Email and number

Adress

Favourite Memory

Guests

Name

Email and number

Address

Favourite Memory

Name

Email and number

Adress

Favourite Memory

Name

Email and number

Adress

Favourite Memory

Guests

Name

Favourite Memory

Email and number

Address

Name

Favourite Memory

Email and number

Adress

Name

Favourite Memory

Email and number

Adress

Guests

Name

Favourite Memory

Email and number

Address

Name

Favourite Memory

Email and number

Adress

Name

Favourite Memory

Email and number

Adress

Guests

Name

Favourite Memory

Email and number

Address

Name

Favourite Memory

Email and number

Adress

Name

Favourite Memory

Email and number

Adress

Guests

Name

Email and number

Address

Favourite Memory

Name

Email and number

Adress

Favourite Memory

Name

Email and number

Adress

Favourite Memory

Notes

Notes

Notes

Notes

Notes

Notes

Notes

Notes

Notes

Notes

Made in the USA
Monee, IL
28 June 2024

60905969R00063